OUR MOTHER TONGUE
ANSWER KEY

OUR MOTHER TONGUE

AN INTRODUCTORY GUIDE TO ENGLISH GRAMMAR

ANSWER KEY

Nancy Wilson

canonpress
Moscow, Idaho

Canon Press
P.O. Box 8729
Moscow, Idaho 83843
800-488-2034 | www.canonpress.com

Nancy Wilson, *Our Mother Tongue: An Introductory Guide to English Grammar: Answer Key*
Copyright © 2004, 2018 by Nancy Wilson

First edition, 2004. Second edition, 2018.

Cover design by James Engerbretson.
Interior Design by Valerie Anne Bost
Printed in the United States of America.
ISBN-13: 978-1-947644-55-7
ISBN-10: 1-947644-55-6

Library of Congress Cataloging-in-Publication Data
Wilson, Nancy
 Our mother tongue / Nancy Wilson.
 p. cm.
Includes index.
1. English language—Grammar—Juvenile literature. 2. English
language—Religious aspects—Christianity—Juvenile literature. I.
Title.
PE1112.W556 2004
428.2—dc21

                                    2003003534

        22 23 24 25   10 9 8 7 6 5 4 3 2

CONTENTS

UNIT 1
THE EIGHT CLASSES OF WORDS

LESSON 1: NOUNS

EXERCISE B

1. crack, rocks, grains, substance, recesses
2. spring, summer, tails, wind, tails, things, will, direction, wind
3. leaves, deal, noise, wind
4. time, tree, wind, tail, creature, appendage, summer-time, peacock, expanse, plumage

EXERCISE E

The nouns of direct address are in italics.

1. "I think myself happy, *King Agrippa*, because today I shall answer for myself." (Acts 26:2)
2. But he said, "I am not mad, *most noble Festus*, but speak the words of truth and reason." (Acts 26:25)
3. Sarah repeated the story her dad told her about Grandpa's Medal of Honor.
4. "But, *Mom*, I didn't know you were here yet."
5. Correct.
6. "I'd like to introduce you, *Mom and Dad*, to my math teacher," said the young man nervously.

LESSON 2: VERBS

EXERCISE D

1. will become
2. seems
3. will be
4. is
5. must be

EXERCISE E

Active verbs, verb phrases, and helping verbs are underlined. Linking verbs are in bold, but should be underlined twice by students.

1. <u>Open</u> your hearts to us. We <u>have wronged</u> no one, we <u>have corrupted</u> no one, we <u>have defrauded</u> no one. (2 Cor. 7:2)
2. Great <u>is</u> my boldness of speech toward you . . . . I **am filled** with comfort. I **am** exceedingly joyful in all our tribulation. (2 Cor. 7:4)
3. But this I <u>say</u>: He who <u>sows</u> sparingly <u>will</u> also <u>reap</u> sparingly, and he who <u>sows</u> bountifully <u>will</u> also <u>reap</u> bountifully. (2 Cor. 9:6)

4. For you <u>know</u> the grace of our Lord Jesus Christ, that thought He <u>was</u> rich, yet for your sakes He <u>became</u> poor, that you through His poverty <u>might become</u> rich. (2 Cor. 8:9)

5. Then Gideon <u>went</u> up by the road of those who <u>dwell</u> in tents on the east of Nobah and Jogbehah; and he <u>attacked</u> the army while the camp <u>felt</u> secure. (Judg. 8:11)

REVIEW EXERCISE A

1. brevity, soul, wit; linking verb: is.
2. boys, tickets, game; verb: were (helping verb) selling.
3. cars, clouds, dust; verbs: raced, raised.
4. woods, colors, autumn; verbs: walked, enjoyed.
5. paint, sides, barn; verbs: was (helping) peeling.

REVIEW EXERCISE B
Nouns

1. houses, advantage, coachmen, chairmen, porters, boys, London (proper), portion.
2. marks, ignorant, shops, signs, aspect, streets.
3. evening, difficulty, danger, walking*, London (proper), windows, pails, regard.
4. falls, bruises, bones, occurrence, year, reign, Charles the Second (proper), streets, darkness.
5. thieves, robbers, trades, impunity, citizens, class, ruffians.
6. amusement, gentlemen, night, town, windows, sedans, men, caresses, women.

* *Walking*, though it can be a verb, is used here to name an activity.

Verbs

1. were numbered, have been, could read.
2. was, (to use†), could understand, were distinguished, gave.
3. closed, became, were opened, were emptied, were passing.
4. were, were left.
5. plied, were.
6. was, (to swagger‡), breaking, upsetting, beating, offering.

LESSON 3: ADJECTIVES

EXERCISE B

1. A, the, blank
2. An, a, a
3. The
4. Blank, a

EXERCISE E

1. quiet, old: town; prettiest: place.
2. long, wide: streets; gigantic, American (proper adjective): elms; drooping: branches; graceful: arches.

† A verb with *to* in front of it is an *infinitive*, and not a verb. Infinitives will be treated in the unit on verbals. In sentence 2, the infinitive *to use* modifies *necessary* as an adverb. In sentence 6, the infinitive *to swagger* is an adjective modifying *amusement*.
‡ A verb with *to* in front of it is an *infinitive*, and not a verb. Infinitives will be treated in the unit on verbals. In sentence 2, the infinitive *to use* modifies *necessary* as an adverb. In sentence 6, the infinitive *to swagger* is an adjective modifying *amusement*.

3. small, gay: flower-gardens; massive: chimney-stacks; protruding: eaves.
4. beautiful: river; tiny: islands.

EXERCISE F

Abbreviations for descriptive adjective (D), limiting adjective (L), possessive adjective (P), definite article (DA), and indefinite article (IA) follow each underlined word in parentheses.

"I remember him as if it were yesterday, as he came plodding to the (DA) inn (D) door, his (P) sea (D)-chest§ following behind him in a (IA) hand (D)-barrow; a (IA) tall (D), strong (D), heavy (D), nut-brown (D) man; his (P) tarry (D) pigtail falling over the (DA) shoulder of his (P) soiled (D) blue (D) coat, his (P) hands ragged (D) and scarred (D), with black (D), broken (D) nails, and the (DA) sabre (D) cut across one (L) cheek, a (IA) dirty (D), livid (D) white (D)."

LESSON 4: ADVERBS

EXERCISE B

Adjectives: The, merry, little, the, tall
Nouns: man, branch, tree
Verbs: sang
Adverbs: cheerily, very

§ Sea-chest and hand-barrow are both compound words. Today *sea chest* is not hyphenated, and *handbarrow* is one word. Although both *sea* and *hand* are descriptive elements, we won't consider them as stand-alone adjectives, but the descriptive part of a compound word.

EXERCISE E

1. *Yesterday*, *today*, and *forever* all modify the adjective *same*. They are all simple adverbs of time.
2. *Out* modifies the verb *went* and is a simple adverb of place. *Quickly* modifies the verb went and is a flexional adverb of manner.
3. *Therefore* modifies the verb *sent*. It is a simple adverb of cause. *More* is a simple adverb of degree modifying the adverb *eagerly* which is a flexional adverb of manner. *Eagerly* also modifies the verb *sent*. *Again* is a simple adverb of time. It modifies the verb *see*. Less is a simple adverb of degree modifying the adjective *sorrowful*.
4. So is a simple adverb of degree which modifies the adverb *loudly*. *Loudly* is a flexional adverb of manner which modifies the verb *shouted*.
5. *Very* is a simple adverb of degree that modifies the adjective *diligent*. *Earnestly* is a flexional adverb of manner that modifies the verb *contend*. *Once for all* is an adverb phrase which means *finally*, so it is an adverb of time. It is modifying the verb *delivered*.
6. *Certainly* is a flexional adverb of affirmation that modifies *not*, which is a simple adverb of negation.
7. *Up* is a simple adverb of place that modifies the verb *go*. *Doubtless* is a simple

adverb of affirmation that modifies the verb phrase *will deliver*.

8. *Never* is a simple adverb of negation modifying the verb phrase *will leave*.

9. So is a simple adverb of degree that modifies the adverb *soon*. *Soon* is a simple adverb of time that modifies the verb phrase *have come*.

10. *Clearly* is a flexional adverb of affirmation modifying the adjective *evident*. *Later* is a simple adverb of time modifying the verb follow.

REVIEW EXERCISE A

Abbreviations for *noun*, *verb*, *adjective*, and *adverb* will follow each word in parentheses.

1. It was (v) a brilliant (adj) moonlit (adj) night (n), but extremely (adv) cold (adj); our (adj) chaise (n) whirled (v) rapidly (adv) over the frozen (adj) ground (n); the noisy (adj) postboy (n) smacked (v) his (adj) long (adj) whip (n) incessantly (adv), and a part (n) of the time (n) his (adj) horses (n) galloped (v).

2. "He knows (v) he is going (v) home,"(adv) said (v) my (adj) companion (n), "and is (v) eager (adj) for some of the merriment (n) and good (adj) cheer (n) of the servants' (adj) hall (n).

3. My (adj) father (n) is (v) a gentleman (n) of the old (adj) school (n), and takes (v) pride (n) in old (adj) English (proper adj) hospitality (n).

4. On our (adj) arrival (n), the squire (n) came (v) out (adv) and received (v) us. He was (v) a fine (adj) , healthy-looking (adj) old (adj) gentleman (n), with silver (adj) hair (n).

5. As the evening (n) was (v) far (adv) advanced (adj), the squire (n) quickly (adv) ushered (v) us into the company (n), which was assembled (v) in a large (adj), old-fashioned (adj) hall (n).

LESSON 5: PRONOUNS

EXERCISE A

1. Jan bought *herself* a set of dishes.
2. *She* later realized that *she* did not need *them* as much as *her* sister Kate did.
3. So *she* gave *them* to *her*.
4. Kate was pleased that Jan had been so generous to *her*.

EXERCISE B

The personal pronouns and possessive pronouns are in italics. The possessive pronouns are followed with an (a) for adjective.

1. Then the chief butler spoke to Pharaoh, saying: "I remember *my* (a) faults this day.
2. When Pharaoh was angry with *his* (a) servants, and put *me* in custody in the house of the captain of the guard, both *me* and the chief baker, *we* each had a dream in one night, *he* and I.

3. Each of *us* dreamed according to the interpretation of *his* (a) own dream.
4. Now there was a young Hebrew man with *us* there, a servant of the captain of the guard.
5. And *we* told *him*, and *he* interpreted *our* (a) dreams for *us*; to each man *he* interpreted according to *his* (a) own dream.
6. And *it* came to pass, just as *he* interpreted for *us*, so *it* happened.
7. *He* restored *me* to *my* (a) office, and *he* hanged *him*."
8. Then Pharaoh sent and called Joseph, and *they* brought *him* quickly out of the dungeon; and *he* shaved, changed *his* (a) clothing, and came to Pharaoh.
9. And Pharaoh said to Joseph, "I have had a dream, and there is no one who can interpret *it*.
10. But I have heard *it* said of *you* that *you* can understand a dream, to interpret *it*."

EXERCISE D

The personal and possessive pronouns are in italics.

1. The first one is done for you.
2. And being assembled together with *them*, *He* commanded *them* not to depart from Jerusalem, but to wait for the Promise of the Father, "which," *He* said, "*you* have heard from *Me*." (Acts 1:4)
   Them: the apostles
   He: Jesus
   Them: the apostles
   He: Jesus

You: the apostles
Me: Jesus

3. Therefore, when *they* had come together, *they* asked *Him* saying, "Lord, will *You* at this time restore the kingdom to Israel?" (v. 6)
   They: the apostles
   Him: Jesus
   You: Jesus
4. And *He* said to *them*, "It is not for *you* to know the times or seasons which the Father has put in *His* own authority." (v. 7)
   He: Jesus
   Them: the apostles
   It: is a substitute for a group of words (the time the Lord will restore the kingdom).
   You: the apostles
   His: God the Father, possessive
5. And suddenly there came a sound from heaven, as of a rushing mighty wind, and *it* filled the whole house where *they* were sitting. (Acts 2:2)
   It: a substitute for a sound like a rushing mighty wind.
   They: the apostles
6. And when this sound occurred, the multitude came together, and were confused, because everyone heard *them* speak in *his* own language. (v. 6)
   Them: the apostles
   His: each of the multitude, possessive
7. But Peter, standing up with the eleven, raised *his* voice and said to *them* . . ."
   (Acts 2:14a)

His: Peter, possessive

Them: the multitude

8. "Men of Israel, hear these words: Jesus of Nazareth, a Man attested by God to *you* by miracles, wonders, and signs which God did through *Him* in *your* midst, as *you yourselves* also know" (v. 22)

    You: the men of Israel

    Him: Jesus

    Your: men of Israel

    You: the men of Israel

    Yourselves: the men of Israel (reflexive)

9. Then those who gladly received *his* word were baptized; and that day about three thousand souls were added to *them*.

    His: Peter, possessive

    Them: the believers

10. (Context is Peter and John praying with their companions.) "For truly against *Your* holy Servant Jesus, whom *You* anointed, both Herod and Pontius Pilate, with the Gentiles and the people of Israel, were gathered together to do whatever *Your* hand and *Your* purpose determined before to be done." (Acts 4:27-28)

    Your: God, possessive

    You: God

    Your: God, possessive

    Your: God, possessive

11. Now Lord, look on *their* threats, and grant to *Your* servants that with all boldness *they* may speak Your word . . . " (v. 29)

Their: Herod, Pontius Pilate, Gentiles, people of Israel, possessive

Your: God, possessive

Your: God, possessive

LESSON 6: PREPOSITIONS

EXERCISE A

The prepositions are italicized below. The objects are underlined.

1. Did you find your homework *in* the <u>car</u>?
2. *After* <u>dinner</u> they went *to* the <u>theater</u>.
3. The child sat *on* her <u>lap</u> *until* <u>bedtime</u>.
4. *Besides* her <u>mother</u>, no one else came to the <u>recital</u>.
5. We've had no rain *since* <u>September</u>.
6. Step *into* the <u>bus</u> quickly.
7. *Without* her <u>textbook</u>, she is lost *in* science <u>class</u>.
8. Go *past* the gas <u>station</u> and turn right *on* <u>Hayes Street</u>.
9. *During* <u>dinner</u> we had three phone calls *from* <u>salesmen</u>.
10. *Throughout* the <u>winter</u> we saw flocks *of* <u>geese</u> flying *over* our <u>house</u>.

EXERCISE C

The object of the prepositions are underlined. Answers will vary. Sample answers:

1. Regarding: She called regarding our <u>move</u>.
2. Despite: I walked home despite the <u>downpour</u>.
3. Beyond: It fell beyond our <u>reach</u>.
4. but (except): All but <u>Susan</u> were absent.
5. During: The alarm sounded during our choir <u>practice</u>.

REVIEW EXERCISE A

All the nouns (n), pronouns (p), verbs (v), adjectives (adj), adverbs (adv), and prepositions (prep) are identified with abbreviations following each.

Now the eyes (n) of (prep) Israel (n) were (v) dim (adj) with (prep) age (n), so that he (p) could (v) not (adv) see (v). Then (adv) Joseph (n) brought (v) them (p) near (prep) him (p), and he (p) kissed (v) them (p) and embraced (v) them (p). So Joseph (n) brought (v) them (p) from (prep) beside (prep) his (adj) knees (n), and he (p) bowed (v) down (adv) with (prep) his (adj) face (n) to (prep) the earth (n). And Joseph (n) took (v) them (p) both, Ephraim (n) with (prep) his (adj) right (adj) hand (n) toward (prep) Israel's (adj) left (adj) hand (n), and Manasseh (n) with (prep) his (adj) left (adj) hand (n) toward (prep) Israel's (adj) right (adj) hand (n), and brought (v) them (p) near (prep) him (p).

LESSON 7: CONJUNCTIONS

EXERCISE C

The conjunctions are in italics and identified as coordinating (cd) or correlative (co).

1. *Both* animals *and* plants live *and* grow. (co/cd)
2. The mother wept, *for* her son was dead. (cd)
3. Thomas sat down, *but* his little sister ran away. (cd)
4. All seek happiness, *yet* not all find it. (cd)
5. *Neither* soldiers *nor* sailors were available to fight. (co)
6. *Whether* you go *or* not does not concern me. (co)
7. They may be slow, *but* they are sure. (cd)
8. *Either* finish your supper *or* excuse yourself from the table. (co)
9. He is *not only* ill, *but* he is *also* weak. (co)
10. Stan *as well as* Dave passed the test. (cd)

LESSON 8: INTERJECTIONS

EXERCISE A

The interjections in the following sentences are italicized.

1. *Quiet!* You should not be talking.
2. *Yikes!* I broke my ankle!
3. *Oh!* I didn't know it was you.
4. *Good heavens!* What a mess you've made.

5. *Wow!* What a beautiful day!

6. *Ouch!* I cut my finger.

EXERCISE B

Interjections are underlined below.

1. And they bowed the knee before Him and mocked Him, saying, "<u>Hail</u>, King of the Jews!" (Mt. 27:29)

2. "<u>Lo</u>, I am with you always." (Mt. 28:20)

3. "<u>Hail</u>, thou that art highly favoured, the Lord is with thee." (Luke 1:28, KJV)

4. Then said I, <u>Ah</u>, Lord God! Behold, I cannot speak, for I am a youth. (Jeremiah 1:6)

5. <u>Alas</u> for the day! for the day of the LORD is at hand, and as a destruction from the Almighty shall it come. (Joel 1:15, KJV)

6. <u>Behold</u>, what manner of love the Father hath bestowed upon us, that we should be called the sons of God. (1 John 3:1, KJV)

7. Assemble and listen, <u>O</u> sons of Jacob, listen to Israel your father. (Genesis 49:2, ESV)

Explanations

1. *Hail* is an interjection used in this sentence as a greeting.

2. *Lo* can be used as an exclamation of joy, grief, surprise, etc. It is a shortened form of *look!*

3. *Hail* is used here also as a greeting.

4. *Ah* is an interjection that can be used to express many different emotions: joy, grief, surprise, pain, disbelief, or pity. What emotion do you think is being expressed in the sentence above?

5. *Alas* expresses great concern, sorrow, or grief.

6. *Behold* is an interjection that simply means *Look!*

7. *O* is an interjection used with solemnity to express many different emotions. In this case, it means, "I am speaking with seriousness, so listen up!"

LESSON 9: REVIEW

ANSWERS TO REVIEW QUESTIONS

NOUNS

1. Name

2. Nomen

3. A word that names a person, place, thing, activity, or idea.

4. Three: common nouns, proper nouns, and nouns of direct address.

5. One's own

6. A word used to name a particular thing, distinguishing it from others in the same class.

7. General

8. Words used to name a general class of things.

9. Answers will vary.

10. Classes of kinds of words

11. Eight

VERBS

1. Word
2. Verbum
3. It is the most important part of the sentence and it comes from the Latin word that literally means *word*.
4. Action verbs, auxiliaries or helping verbs, and linking verbs.
5. A linking verb is used to join two words, and can be recognized by substituting the word *is* or an equal sign with the verb.
6. An auxiliary helps another verb assert something. Another name for an auxiliary verb is helping verb.

ADJECTIVES

1. That can add to.
2. Adjectus.
3. An adjective modifies a word by describing, qualifying, or limiting it.
4. A noun or pronoun.
5. Which? What kind? How many? Whose? How much?
6. Answers will vary.
7. Adjectives used to limit a noun.
8. Joint or knuckle.
9. A or *an* comes from the Saxon word for one. *The* comes from the word for that.
10. Definite and indefinite.

ADVERBS

1. They are words added to verbs.
2. It comes from the words *ad* and *verbum*.
3. An adverb modifies a verb, adjective, or another adverb.
4. How? Where? When? To what extent?

PRONOUNS

1. It means for a name.
2. Pro nomen
3. A word which is used to replace a noun or a name.
4. The antecedent
5. It comes from the Latin *ante* and *cedere*, which mean to go before, and in this case it goes before the pronoun.
6. Personal, reflexive, and possessive.
7. I, me, myself, we, us, ourselves, you, yourself, yourselves, he, him, himself, she, her, herself, it, itself, they, them, themselves.
8. Personal pronouns take the place of names of persons.

PREPOSITIONS

1. Placed before.
2. Praepositus
3. Thye are used to connect words and show relation between them. They are usually placed before another word called the object of the preposition.
4. Answers will vary.
5. A noun or pronoun that follows a preposition.

CONJUNCTIONS

1. It means to join together.
2. Conjungo
3. Conjunctions are words that join or connect words, groups of words, or sentences.
4. And, or, but, for, nor
5. Coordinating conjunctions connect grammatically equal words, groups of words, or sentences; correlative conjunctions do the same, but always come in pairs.

INTERJECTIONS

1. It means thrown between.
2. Interjectus
3. A word (or group of words) used as a sudden expression of feeling or emotion that is not grammatically connected to the sentence.
4. Answers will vary.
5. A short part of speech that connects, limits, or shows relationship. It includes articles, conjunctions, interjections, and prepositions.

EXERCISE A

1. The (adj) LORD (n) is (v) my (adj) shepherd (n); I (p) shall (v) not (adv) want (v).
2. He (p) makes (v) me (p) (to) lie (v) down (adv) in (prep) green (adj) pastures (n).
3. He (p) leads (v) me (p) beside (prep) the (adj) still (adj) waters (n).
4. He (p) restores (v) my (adj) soul (n).
5. He (p) leads (v) me (p) in (prep) the (adj) paths (n) of (prep) righteousness (n) for (prep) His (adj) name's (adj) sake (n).

EXERCISE D

1. James (n) writes (v) very (adv) well (adv).
2. The (adj) Apostles (n) preached (v) the (adj) gospel (n).
3. Jesus Christ (n) was (v) rich (adj), yet (con) He (p) became (v) poor (adj).
4. The (adj) Scriptures (n) teach (v) love (n) to (prep) God (n) and (con) man (n).
5. Good (adj) and (con) wise (adj) men (n) make (v) valuable (adj) friends (n).
6. A (adj) wise (adj) son (n) hears (v) the (adj) instructions (n) of (prep) a (adj) father (n).
7. Envy (n) and (con) anger (n) cause (v) great (adj) pain (n), and (con) they (p) shorten (v) life (n).
8. Anger (n) rests (v) in (prep) the (adj) bosom (n) of (prep) wicked (adj) men (n).
9. A (adj) good (adj) man (n) dismisses (v) all (adj) unkind (adj) feelings (n).
10. Death (n) to (prep) good (adj) men (n) is (v) the (adj) gate (n) of (prep) Heaven (n).
11. A (adj) hospital (n) is (v) a (adj) place (n) where* (adv) sick (adj) persons (n) are (v) received (v).

* *Where* is an adverb introducing an adjective clause. These will be covered in a later lesson.

12. A (adj) thoughtful (adj) mind (n) will (v) find (v) instruction (n) in (prep) all (adj) things (n).

13. God (n) has (v) shown (v) love (n) to (prep) man (n), though† man (n) returns (v) it (p) not (adv).

14. We (p) defer (v) repentance (n) to (prep) some (adj) future (adj) time (n), because‡ we (p) love (v) sin (n).

15. In (prep) books (n) we (p) find (v) much (adj) valuable (adj) instruction (n).

EXERCISE E

Nouns in the following paragraph are identified as common or proper (c or pr), singular or plural (s or pl), and abstract or concrete (a or cc).

1. Sam Gamgee married Rose Cotton in the spring . . . and they came and lived at Bag End.

   Sam Gamgee: pr, s, cc

   Rose Cotton: pr, s, cc

   Spring: c, s, a

   Bag End: pr, s, cc

2. And if Sam thought himself lucky, Frodo knew that he was more lucky himself; for there was not a hobbit in the Shire that was looked after with such care.

   Sam: pr, s, cc

   Frodo: pr, s, cc

   Hobbit: c, s, cc

   Shire: pr, s, cc

   Care: c, s, a

3. When the labors or repair had all been planned and set going he took to a quiet life, writing . . . and going through all his notes.

   Labors: c, pl, a

   Repair: c, s, a

   Life: c, s, a

   Notes: c, pl, cc

4. He resigned the office of Deputy Mayor at the Free Fair that Midsummer, and dear old Will Whitfoot had another seven years of presiding at Banquets.

   Office: c, s, a

   Deputy Mayor: pr, s, a

   Free Fair: pr, s, a

   Midsummer: pr, s, a

   Will Whitfoot: pr, s, c

   Years: c, pl, a

   Banquets: pr (since it is capitalized), pl, a

† *Though* is a subordinating conjunction. These will be covered in a later lesson.

‡ *Because* is another subordinating conjunction.

UNIT 2
THE SENTENCE

LESSON 10: KINDS OF SENTENCES

EXERCISE B

1. The farmers are harvesting the wheat. (Declarative)
2. Tell me what you are thinking. (Imperative)
3. Where are you going after class? (Interrogative)
4. How dark the sky is! (Exclamatory)
5. Call my brother back. (Imperative, and with an exclamation point, also Exclamatory)
6. My locker is very full of books. (Declarative)
7. His birthday is next month. (Declarative)
8. What is the answer to question number four? (Interrogative)
9. Be quiet. (Imperative, and with an exclamation point, also Exclamatory)
10. What a day I've had! (Exclamatory)

EXERCISE C

1. The bonfire burned brightly.
   Did the bonfire burn brightly?
   Let the bonfire burn brightly.
   How brightly the bonfire burns!
2. The morning flew by.
   Did the morning fly by?
   Let the morning fly by.
   How the morning flew by!
3. The wind blew fiercely.
   Did the wind blow fiercely?
   Let the wind blow fiercely.
   How fiercely the wind blows!
4. The students read eagerly.
   Do the students read eagerly?
   Let the students read eagerly.
   How eagerly the students read!
5. The wedding was lovely.
   Was the wedding lovely?
   Let it be a lovely wedding.
   What a lovely wedding!

EXERCISE D

1. Imperative
2. Imperative

3. Imperative
4. Imperative
5. Imperative
6. Declarative
7. Declarative
8. Imperative
9. Imperative
10. Declarative

LESSON 11: THE SUBJECT

EXERCISE A

In the following exercises the subjects are italicized.

1. A *band* was playing in the park.
2. The football *game* was canceled.
3. *She* showed me her photographs.
4. *We* rode home.
5. The *sunset* was glorious.

EXERCISE B

In the following exercises the subjects are italicized.

1. *Dogs* and *cats* are America's favorite pets.
2. The *students* and *parents* gathered for school orientation.
3. My *shelf* is full of my favorite books.
4. *Robinson Crusoe* and *Pilgrim's Progress* are among them.
5. *Ketchup*, *mayonnaise*, and *mustard* were served with the hamburgers.

EXERCISE C

The subjects in the sentences below are italicized.

1. The first one is done for you.
2. The second one is done for you.
3. The third one is done for you.
4. The fourth one is done for you.
5. At the doorstep on summer evenings sat the little stray *dog*.
6. A *noun* or a *pronoun* can be used as a subject.
7. *Adjectives* and *adverbs* are called modifiers.
8. Up into the clouds went the *balloon* and *string*.
9. What bright blue eyes *she* has!
10. In the dark shade of the forest stands an old *house* and a weather-beaten *barn*.
11. Are *Sue* and *David* coming to dinner tonight?
12. Three little *girls* were giggling in the corner.
13. *Sam* and *Judy* will be here soon.
14. *Latin* and *literature* are his favorite classes this year.

EXERCISE F

The subjects are underlined in the following sentences.

1. The first-place <u>prize</u> was awarded to Dave and Samuel. (blank)
2. Their <u>boat</u> came in first, and <u>second-place</u> was a tie. (Cd-Sen)
3. In the early hours of a spring morning, the <u>robins</u> and the <u>pheasants</u> make a cheerful racket. (Cd-Subj)

4. The <u>students</u> and <u>teachers</u> gathered in the auditorium for the meeting. (Cd-Subj)

5. The <u>lecture</u> went long, and the <u>students</u> got drowsy. (Cd-Sen)

LESSON 12: THE PREDICATE

EXERCISE C

1. Dogs growl.

2. Boys are watching.

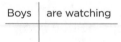

3. Teams are competing.

4. Houses have been built.

Houses | have been built

5. I am studying.

EXERCISE D

1. Poplars and willows were planted.

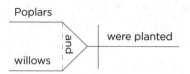

2. Dave and Jill are touring and traveling.

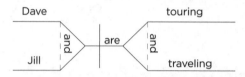

3. Mom and Dad are walking and jogging.

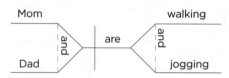

4. Men, women, and children rushed through the gates and filled the courtyard.

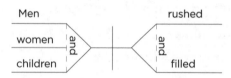

5. Camels, donkeys, carts, and bicycles moved slowly along the dusty road.

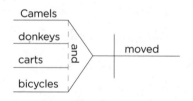

LESSON 13:
THE SUBJECT MODIFIED BY AN ADJECTIVE

EXERCISE B

1. She has an old, old necklace that was her grandmother's.
2. Sam wrote a clear, precise, intelligent essay that won him the prize.
3. His classmates viewed him as reserved and proud, ambitious and haughty.
4. The tired, drooping, hungry preschoolers toddled off the bus.
5. He drove a shiny, new, bright red pickup in the parade.

EXERCISE C

1. His old family Bible was treasured.

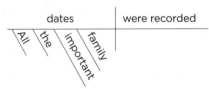

2. Several favorite passages were underlined.

passages	were underlined

3. All the important family dates were recorded.

dates	were recorded

4. The black leather cover was cracking.

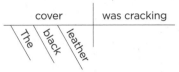

cover	was cracking

5. The well-worn, thin pages crackled.

pages	crackled

6. The gold lettering shone.

lettering	shone

7. Many family names were inscribed.

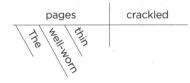

names	were inscribed

LESSON 14:
THE SUBJECT MODIFIED BY A POSSESSIVE NOUN

EXERCISE A

1. Child's, prince's, baby's, teacher's, uncle's.
2. Father's, cat's, John's, dog's, mercy's.
3. Bible's, verse's, painter's, sister's, house's.
4. Charles's, Jesus', princess's, bridge's, foxes'.
5. Williamses', Xerxes', Davis's, geese's.

EXERCISE B

1. His book was finished!

book	was finished

His

2. Their names were announced.

names	were announced

Their

3. The child's mother called.

mother	called

The / child's

4. The Bible's cover was missing.

cover	was missing

The / Bible's

5. Her aunt was visiting.

aunt	was visiting

Her

LESSON 15:
THE SUBJECT MODIFIED BY AN APPOSITIVE

EXERCISE A

The appositives and appositive phrases are italicized in the sentences below.

1. David, *the psalmist*, was a man after God's own heart.

2. Our faithful dog, *a golden retriever*, guards the house.

3. My father, *a veteran of World War II*, has several medals for heroism.

4. *A fine student and leader*, Sam will go places.

5. *My daughter* Sarah is my best friend.*
   (It is possible to identify *daughter* as the noun modified and *Sarah* as the appositive.)

EXERCISE B

1. Mr. Gibbs, the new science teacher, will speak at the assembly today.

2. The new library, a beautiful brick building, will be quite an asset to the community.

3. The boys' piano teacher, Mrs. Williams, will come for supper tonight.

4. Latin, a language considered dead by many people, is the source of over half of English vocabulary.

5. Jim Miller, the new boy on the team, came from Texas.

EXERCISE C

1. My favorite book, *Pride and Prejudice*, has been reviewed.

book (Pride and Prejudice)	has been reviewed

My / favorite

2. The library, an old historic building, will be demolished.

library (building)	will be demolished

The / an / old / historic

3. Her puppy, a chocolate lab, is barking.

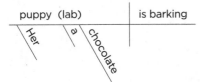

4. The boss's lunch, a sub sandwich, is missing.

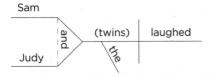

5. Sam and Judy, the twins, laughed!

6. The Constitution, an important national document, is guarded.

7. The delivery man, my neighbor, is coming.

8. Roast beef, our favorite dinner, will be provided.

9. My alarm clock, a royal nuisance, was destroyed.

10. The popular coffee shop, her perpetual hangout, closed.

LESSON 16: THE PREPOSITIONAL PHRASE USED AS AN ADJECTIVE

EXERCISE A

Example adjective phrases are given below.

1. The storm blew down a barn in the neighborhood.
2. A table of oak fills the dining room.
3. Women of virtue are pleasing to God.
4. We listened to a speech about history.
5. She is a woman with sense.

EXERCISE B

The adjective phrases are italicized and the nouns they modify are underlined.

1. A <u>house</u> *of stone* is not uncommon in England.
2. A <u>tourist</u> *from Australia* visited us last week.

3. <u>Roads</u> *in the country* are muddy in the spring.

4. <u>Grapes</u> *from California* make fine wine.

5. The <u>car</u> *with the broken headlight* is mine.

EXERCISE D

1. The princess from a faraway land was kidnapped.

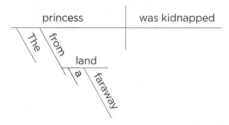

2. A prince on a white stallion arrived.

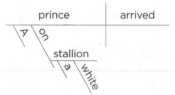

3. His kind offer of rescue was accepted.

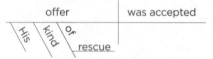

4. The saddle upon his white stallion slipped.

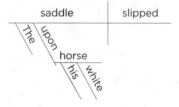

5. The look on the face of the princess changed.

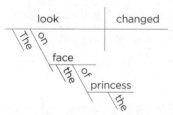

6. The prince's grip on the horse prevailed.

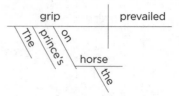

7. The tale of happiness and adventure began.

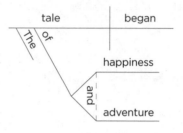

LESSON 17: THE SUBJECT MODIFIED BY AN ADJECTIVE CLAUSE

EXERCISE A

The adjective clause is in italics, the noun modified is underlined, and the relative pronoun is bold.

1. <u>He</u> **who** *heeds the word wisely* will find good.

2. There is a <u>way</u> **that** *seems right to a man,* but its end is the way of death.

3. <u>He</u> **who** *has knowledge* spares his words, and a man of understanding is of a calm spirit.

4. Better is the <u>poor</u> **who** *walks in his integrity* than <u>one</u> **who** *is perverse in his lips,* and is a fool.

5. <u>Blows</u> **that** *hurt* cleanse away evil.

EXERCISE C

The adjective clauses are italicized.

1. This is the room *where we will have the reception.*
2. Here is the book *I bought.*
3. That is the reason *why I am late.*
4. May is the month *when he will graduate.*
5. Now is the time *when we should go.*

EXERCISE D

1. The package that is in the hall is moving.

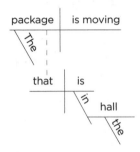

2. The vase which fell shattered.

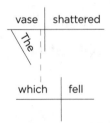

3. The prize which was promised arrived.

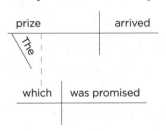

4. The boy who laughed was corrected.

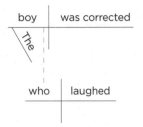

5. The man apologized to the woman whose fender he had dented.

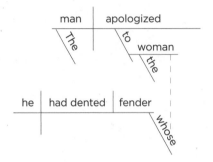

LESSON 18: THE PREDICATE MODIFIED BY AN ADVERB

EXERCISE A

1. I *politely* but *firmly* told the salesman I was *not* interested.
2. He *resolutely* continued with his sales pitch.
3. I *calmly* told my daughter the news.
4. He said he would call *tomorrow*, but he *never* did.
5. She is climbing *down now.*

EXERCISE B

1. The small child cried angrily.

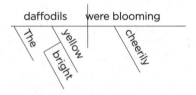

2. The bright yellow daffodils were blooming cheerily.

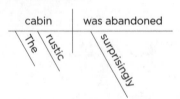

3. Several small boys were playing noisily.

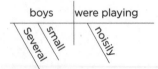

4. The rustic cabin was surprisingly abandoned.

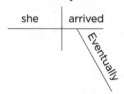

5. Today he suddenly left.

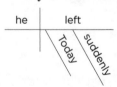

6. First she exercised.

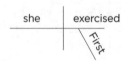

7. Next she read.

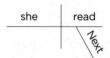

8. Finally she breakfasted and left.

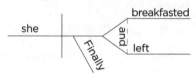

9. Eventually, she arrived.

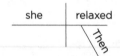

10. Then she relaxed.

LESSON 19: THE PREPOSITIONAL PHRASE USED AS AN ADVERB

EXERCISE A

The adverb phrases are italicized in the sentences below.

1. A basket of goodies sat *by the door*.
2. *From the window* of the train we saw an old brick schoolhouse.
3. Man shall not live *by bread* alone.
4. She arrived *at London in the morning* and stayed *for two days*.

5. We waited *for him for several minutes*, but we left *in a hurry*.
6. The dog jumped *over the fence in pursuit* of the cat.
7. Wait *on the Lord*.
8. The youngster confided *in his mother about his hopes* for a Christmas gift.
9. The track team ran *around the track in the pouring rain*.
10. *From the roof* we can see *beyond the mountains*.

EXERCISE B

1. The streets in Moscow are covered with snow.

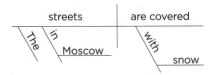

2. A toddler with his mother's purse wandered out the door and into the yard.

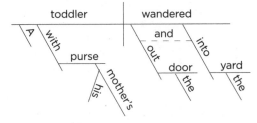

3. In early spring many tulips bloom in the park on the campus.

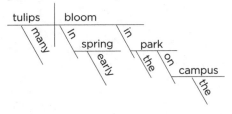

4. They shopped at the mall for several hours.

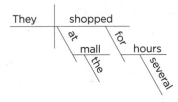

5. Thousands of stars appeared in the sky.

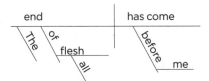

6. The end of all flesh has come before Me. (Gen. 6:13)

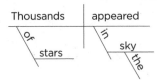

7. Then the men turned away from there and went toward Sodom. (Gen. 18:22)

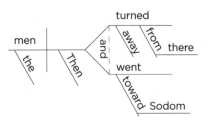

8. The evil will bow before the good. (Prov. 14:19)

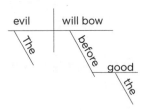

9. The wrath of God is revealed from heaven against all ungodliness and unrighteousness of men. (Rom. 1:18)

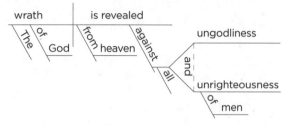

10. Mercy triumphs over judgment. (James 2:13)

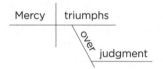

5. She set the vase of flowers <u>where</u> *we all could see it.*

6. <u>When</u> *you are ready for us,* call us.

7. <u>After</u> *she had washed the crystal,* she gently set it in the hutch.

8. She polished the silver <u>because</u> *it was tarnished quite badly.*

9. <u>As soon as</u> *he finished his test,* he smiled with relief.

10. He ran with the ball <u>as though</u> *he were going for a touchdown.*

LESSON 20: THE PREDICATE MODIFIED BY AN ADVERB CLAUSE

EXERCISE A

The adverb clauses are in italics, and the subordinate conjunctions are underlined.

1. Mom sewed on my dress <u>while</u> *I watched the little ones.*

2. The sky looked <u>as if</u> *it might rain any minute.*

3. <u>Wherever</u> *I walked in the garden,* I only saw more splendid sights.

4. Susan brought Sam home <u>so that</u> *we could meet him.*

EXERCISE C

1. David looks as though he already knew.

2. We will go if the team wins.

3. You should read whenever you can.

4. Unless he arrives soon, the game will be canceled.

5. As soon as you finish, I will begin.

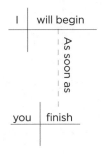

6. While he was still speaking with them, Rachel came with her father's sheep. (Genesis 29:9)

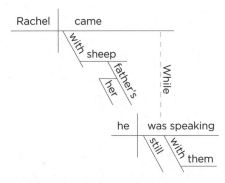

7. Though his hatred is covered by deceit, His wickedness will be revealed before the assembly. (Proverbs 26:26)

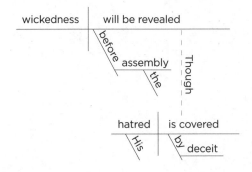

8. Although I heard, I did not understand. (Daniel 12:8)

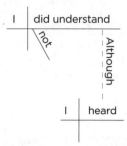

9. After I have been raised, I will go before you to Galilee. (Matthew 26:32)

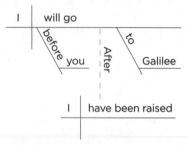

10. I will sing to the LORD, because He has dealt bountifully with me. (Psalm 13:6)

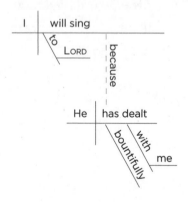

LESSON 21: THE PREDICATE WITH A DIRECT OBJECT

EXERCISE A

The direct objects in the sentences below are in italics.

1. Ben kicked the *ball* across the field for a goal.
2. You hit the *nail* on the head!
3. He pushed the *sofa* to the den.
4. She lost her *purse*.
5. Mom wrote a *check* for their trip.
6. He's reading A Tale of Two Cities for literature class.
7. She bought six new *trees* for the yard.
8. The band played several *songs* from the forties.
9. I could not read the *sign* in the dark.
10. He loaded the *luggage* into the trunk of the car.

EXERCISE B

1. The church choir sang Christmas carols at the concert.

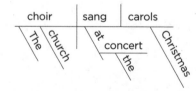

2. She pasted a stamp on the envelope.

3. The child licked the lollipop joyously.

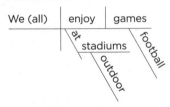

4. He opened the letter nervously.

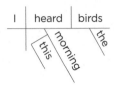

5. We all enjoy football games at outdoor stadiums.

6. She reached the meeting on time.

7. They attended their aunt's funeral in June.

8. The committee sent their findings.

9. The new teacher wrote her name on the board.

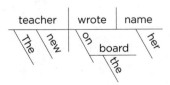

10. I heard the birds this morning.

EXERCISE C

The verbs and helping verbs from Psalm 23 are underlined and abbreviations for transitive (T) and intransitive (I) follow in parentheses. Direct objects are italicized.

1. The LORD <u>is</u> (I) my shepherd.
2. I <u>shall</u> not <u>want (I)</u>.
3. He <u>leads</u> (T) *me* beside still waters.
4. He <u>restores</u> (T) my *soul.*
5. I <u>will fear</u> (T) no *evil.*
6. You <u>prepare</u> (T) a *table* before me in the presence of my enemies.
7. You <u>anoint</u> (T) my *head* with oil.
8. My cup <u>runs</u> (I) over.
9. Surely goodness and mercy <u>shall follow</u> (T) *me* all the days of my life.
10. And I <u>will dwell</u> (I) in the house of the LORD forever.

LESSON 22:
THE PREDICATE WITH
AN INDIRECT OBJECT

EXERCISE A

The indirect objects are underlined; the direct objects are in italics.

1. The company gave the <u>school</u> a large *grant* for computers.
2. The instructor handed the <u>students</u> a long reading *list*.
3. You promised <u>me</u> your cookie *recipe*.
4. Give <u>Charles</u> my *greeting*.
5. She sang the <u>baby</u> a *lullaby*.
6. Mother baked the <u>senior class</u> a *cake* for their graduation party.
7. My sister made <u>me</u> a velvet *dress*.
8. The babysitter read the <u>children</u> a *story*.
9. I ordered <u>myself</u> a new *desk*.
10. We poured <u>Mother</u> some *tea*.

EXERCISE B

1. The baby gave me a smile.

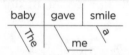

2. Mom sent the college a letter of recommendation.

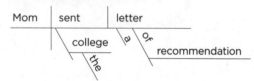

3. He gave the class a long lecture.

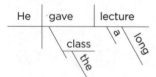

4. My host ordered me a cocktail.

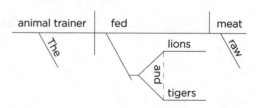

5. The hostess handed me a napkin.

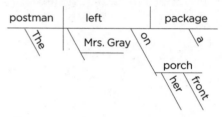

6. The guests took her flowers.

7. The postman left Mrs. Gray a package on her front porch.

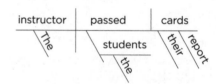

8. The instructor passed the students their report cards.

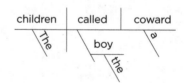

9. The children called the boy a coward.

10. The animal trainer fed the lions and tigers raw meat.

LESSON 23:
THE PREDICATE WITH A PREDICATE NOMINATIVE

EXERCISE A

The predicate nominatives in the sentences below are in italics.

1. Raphael was an *artist*.
2. The whale is the largest *mammal*.
3. Tadpoles become *frogs*.
4. Faithfulness is a *virtue*.
5. The Church is the *bride* of Christ.
6. The boy was a *dunce*.
7. Lewis and Clark were famous *explorers*.
8. Jeremy is a fine *athlete*.
9. The moon is not a *star*.
10. The boy is my *nephew*.

EXERCISE C

The predicate nominatives in these sentences are in italics.

1. Children are a *heritage* from the LORD.
2. The fruit of the womb is His *reward*.
3. Your children are olive *plants* around your table.
4. Your wife shall be a fruitful *vine*.
5. My soul is a weaned *child* within me.
6. The idols of the nations are *silver* and *gold*.
7. Their tongues are *serpents* full of poison.
8. You are my *refuge*, O LORD.
9. You are my *portion* in the land of the living.

10. The LORD is the *One* who gives salvation to kings.

EXERCISE D

1. My favorite herb is rosemary.

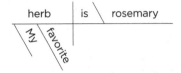

2. Susie's brother is an attorney.

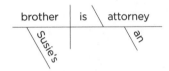

3. My favorite sport is basketball.

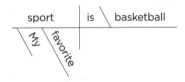

4. This is our new teacher.

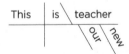

5. That was her best race.

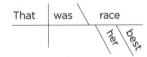

6. Children are a heritage from the LORD.

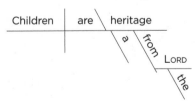

7. The fruit of the womb is His reward.

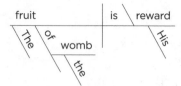

8. Your children are olive plants around your table.

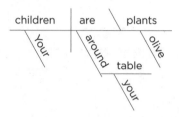

9. Your wife shall be a fruitful vine.

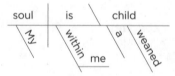

10. My soul is a weaned child within me.

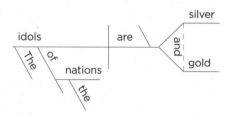

11. The idols of the nations are silver and gold.

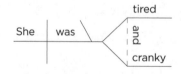

LESSON 24: THE PREDICATE WITH A PREDICATE ADJECTIVE

EXERCISE A

The predicate adjectives in the sentences below are in italics.

1. He is *happy* who has the God of Jacob for his help.
2. The LORD is *righteous*.
3. LORD, my heart is not *haughty*; my eyes are not *lofty*.
4. The LORD is *good* to all.
5. Your tabernacle is *lovely*, O LORD of Hosts!
6. That fragrance smells *sweet*.
7. Do not be *unwise*.
8. He is *worthy* of the honor.
9. The owl looks *wise*.
10. The children seemed *happy*.

EXERCISE C

1. She was tired and cranky.

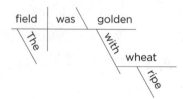

2. The field was golden with ripe wheat.

field | was \ golden
The / with / wheat / ripe

3. The air smells fresh and clean.

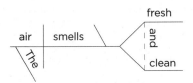

4. The young man seemed honest and upright.

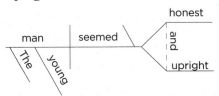

5. The puppy was soft and cuddly.

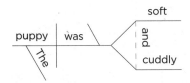

6. This plum tastes terrible.

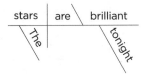

7. The stars are brilliant tonight.

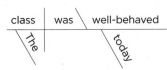

8. You are wrong.

You | are \ wrong

9. The class was well-behaved today.

class | was \ well-behaved ... The ... today

10. The snow became slushy quickly.

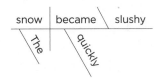

REVIEW EXERCISE A

Each of the complements in the following sentences is underlined and followed by abbreviations for direct object (DO), indirect object (IO), predicate nominative (PN), and predicate adjective (PA) in parentheses.

1. Examine me (DO), O Lord, and prove me (DO); Try my mind (DO) and my heart (DO). (Ps. 26:2)
2. I have hated the assembly (DO) of evildoers. (Ps. 26:5)
3. I will wash my hands (DO) in innocence. (Ps. 26:6)
4. The Lord is my light (PN) and my salvation (PN); Whom (DO) shall I fear? (Ps. 27:1)
5. The Lord is the strength (PN) of my life. (Ps. 27:1)
6. Teach me (IO) Your way (DO), O Lord. (Ps. 27:11)
7. Blessed (PA) be the Lord. (Ps. 28:6)
8. The Lord is their strength (PN), And He is the saving refuge (PN) of His anointed. (Ps. 28:8)
9. The voice of the Lord is powerful (PA); the voice of the Lord is full (PA) of majesty. (Ps. 29:3)
10. The Lord will give strength (DO) to His people; The Lord will bless His people (DO) with peace. (Ps. 28:11)

LESSON 25:
THE NOUN CLAUSE

EXERCISE A

The noun clauses in the following sentences are in italics. They are identified in parentheses as subject (S), direct object (DO), object of the preposition (OP), predicate nominative (PN), or appositive (App) in the sentence.

1. I know *what you want.* (DO)
2. The fact *that the roof leaks* is the reason for the low price. (App)
3. *Whether it rains or snows* never affects her travel plans. (S)
4. *Whoever applies for the job* will be considered. (S)
5. The teacher said *that our tests were graded.* (DO)
6. *Why you bought tickets to Alaska* is beyond me. (S)
7. The lawn will be watered by *whoever housesits for us.* (OP)
8. The reason for the notice is *that he hasn't paid his bill.* (PN)
9. I must write Mother about *how she sang.* (OP)
10. She told me *that she had already called you.* (DO)

EXERCISE B

In the following sentences noun, adjective, and adverb clauses are italicized and identified.

1. *Whenever I travel* (adv), I pack only *what I absolutely need* (n)
2. No one knows *whether he is going to school in the fall* (n)
3. Experienced travelers, *who must travel frequently for their jobs* (adj), usually know *where the best deals are* (n)
4. The flight *that we took from San Francisco* (adj) was very crowded
5. *Because the flight was so long* (adv), I felt very groggy *when we arrived* (adv)
6. The meal *that they served* (adj) wasn't bad
7. *That we made it safely home* (n) was my chief desire
8. I don't know *how long I slept* (n)
9. One of the complaints about the food was *that it was cold* (n)
10. *When the wind blows at our house* (adv), the windows shake

EXERCISE C

1. I heard that you have lost your watch.

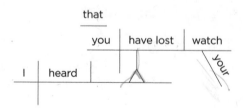

2. I know they will do what is right.

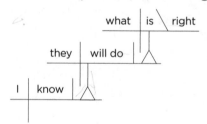

3. That they lost the first two games did not discourage them.

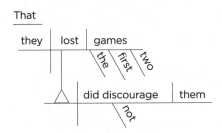

4. I bet his plane will be late.

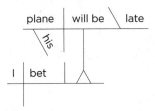

5. The truth is that I am exhausted.

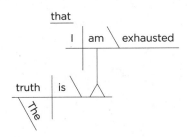

6. I will give you whatever is fair.

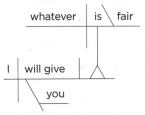

7. What his plans are will be a surprise.

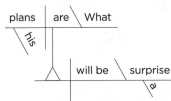

8. That some pages are missing is a problem with the book.

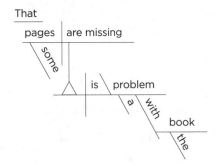

9. Invite whomever you want.

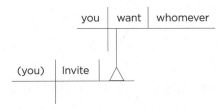

10. The buildings will be painted by whomever he hires for the summer.

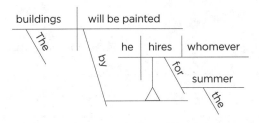

REVIEW EXERCISE A

The noun clauses are underlined in the following sentences, and the connective words are in bold.

1. **Why** he decided to buy the pony is a mystery to me!

2. **Whether** you come or not will affect my decision.

3. **Where** the movie is showing is not the point of my concern.

4. <u>**Whoever** made these delicious cookies deserves a prize!</u>

5. <u>**What** happened at breakfast</u> caused us to be late.

6. He told her <u>**where** he grew up</u>.

7. We believe <u>**that** Jesus rose from the dead</u>.

8. The dog chased <u>**whoever** walked by his yard</u>.

9. He asked <u>**why** he had to do his homework</u>.

10. John asked his dad <u>**whose** new car was parked in the driveway</u>.

11. Please return the keys to <u>**whoever** lost them</u>.

12. The cat climbed to <u>**where** it couldn't be reached</u>.

13. She looked at <u>**what** the storm had done</u>.

14. The customer waited for <u>**what** he had ordered</u>.

15. She slipped the money to <u>**where** he couldn't see it</u>.

16. Her life-long dream is <u>**that** she can meet her relatives in Scotland</u>.

17. He became <u>**what** his parents had predicted</u>.

18. You are <u>**what** you eat</u>.

19. Her one regret was <u>**that** she failed math</u>.

20. A wise man is <u>**what** I want to be</u>.

REVIEW EXERCISE B

Answers will vary.

LESSON 26: SENTENCE STRUCTURE

EXERCISE A

1. He has regarded the lowly state of His maidservant. (v. 48)

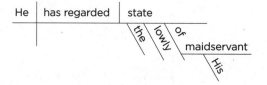

2. He has done great things for me. (v. 49)

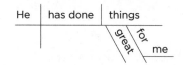

3. Holy is His name. (v. 49)

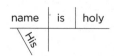

4. He has shown strength with His arm. (v. 51)

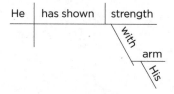

5. He has put down* the mighty from their thrones. (v. 52)

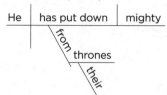

* *Put down* is a phrasal verb.

6. Mary remained with her about three months, and returned to her house. (v. 56)

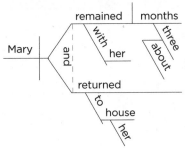

EXERCISE B

1. My soul magnifies the Lord, and my spirit has rejoiced in God my Savior† . (Luke 1:46-47)

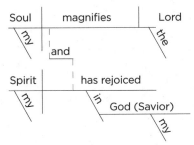

2. He has done great things for me, and holy is His name. (v. 49)

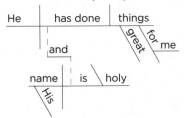

3. He has put down the mighty from their thrones, and He has exalted the lowly. (v. 52)

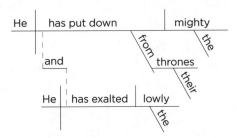

4. He has filled the hungry with good things, and the rich He has sent away‡ empty. (v. 53)

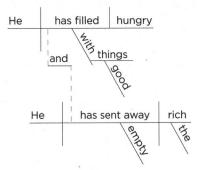

5. Mary remained with her about three months, and she returned to her house. (v. 56)

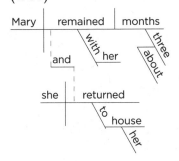

EXERCISE C

1. The teachers and the students gathered in the gym.

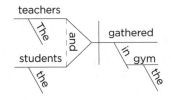

† *Savior* is an appositive.

‡ *Sent away* is another phrasal verb.

2. The basketball sailed across the gym and slipped through the basket.

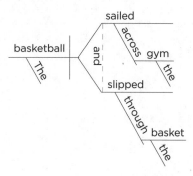

3. The freshmen and sophomores jumped from their seats and cheered wildly.

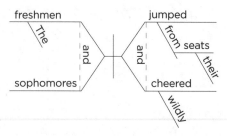

4. My brother, Michael, won a college scholarship.

5. The little boy with the dog passes my house every day.

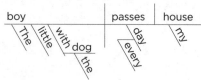

6. He walks along the sidewalk and whistles for the dog.

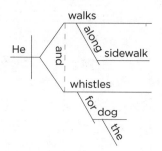

7. a. The gift that I bought yesterday is lost.

b. The student who finishes first will get extra credit.

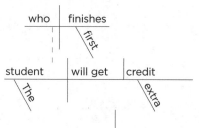

8. a. After I finished my homework, I enjoyed my evening.

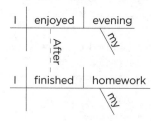

b. She will call me when her plane arrives.

9. Please bring the mail into my office.

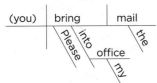

10. Dad brought Mom a bouquet of roses for their anniversary.

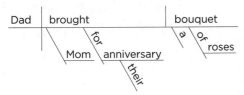

11. My brother, who lives in Wyoming, is a cardiologist.

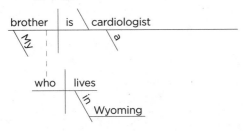

12. Since I wrote a cookbook for kids, I have become rich and famous.

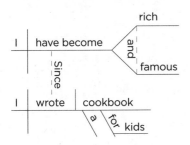

13. a. He told me that he loves his job.

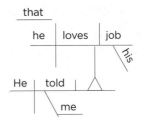

b. The day that he became president of the golf club was the turning point of his life.

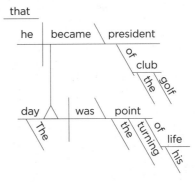

14. The hobbits huddled around the fire, and they could see orcs in the distance.

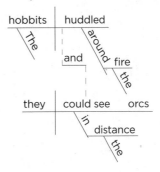

15. If you want my opinion, you can call me.

16. As they reached the forest, they ran for shelter, and the enemy did not see them.

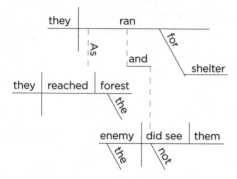

EXERCISE D

1. When you leave for school today, wear your boots.

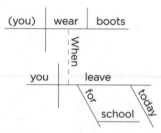

2. Because heavy snow fell overnight, school was canceled.

3. David Rutherford, who won the speech contest, will speak at the graduation.

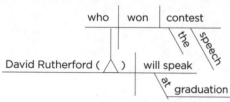

EXERCISE E

1. When they had crossed over, they came to the land of Gennesaret, and they anchored there.

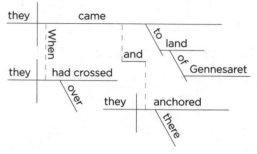

2. Wherever He entered, into villages, cities, or the country, they laid the sick in the marketplaces, and they begged Him that they might just touch the border of his garment.

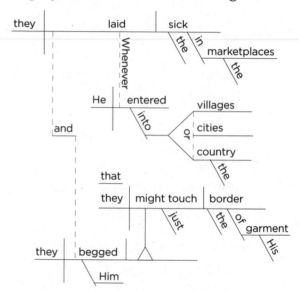

EXERCISE F

The following sentences are identified as simple (s), compound (cd), complex (cx), or compound-complex (cd-cx).

1. A righteous man who falters before the wicked is like a murky spring and a polluted well (Prov. 25:26). cx

2. He who gives a right answer kisses the lips (Prov. 24:26). cx

3. He who covers his sin will not prosper (Prov. 28:13a). cx

4. Do not forsake your own friend or your father's friend, nor go to your brother's house in the day of your calamity (Prov. 27:10a). s

5. Whoever walks blamelessly will be saved, but he who is perverse in his ways will suddenly fall (Prov. 28:18). cd-cx

6. When Jesus departed from there, two blind men followed Him, crying out. (Mt. 9:27) cx

7. Seeing the multitudes, He went up on a mountain. (Mt. 5:1) cx

8. I worship the God of my fathers, believing all things which are written in the Law and in the Prophets. (Acts 24:14) cx

9. The statutes of the LORD are right, rejoicing the heart. (Ps. 19:8) cx

10. The commandment of the LORD is pure, enlightening the eyes. (Ps. 19:8) cx

EXERCISE G

1. Who can find a virtuous wife?

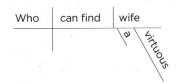

2. The heart of her husband safely trusts her; So he will have no lack of gain.

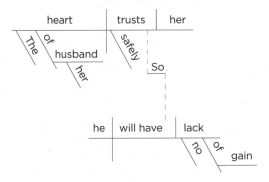

3. She seeks wool and flax, and willingly works with her hands.

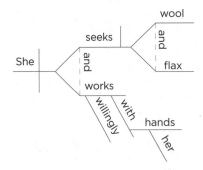

4. She also rises while it is yet night, and provides food for her household and a portion for her maidservants.

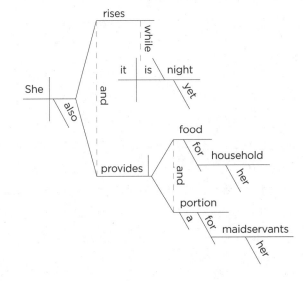

5. Her husband is known in the gates when he sits among the elders of the land.

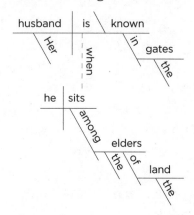

LESSON 27: REVIEW

EXERCISE A

Suggestions for adjectives (or possessive nouns) are in parentheses.

The (Mom's, old) swing gently rocked in the wind.

My (new) car needs repairs.

The (big, gray) clouds covered the mountain.

Examples in parentheses.

1. The swing (on the porch) gently rocked in the wind.
2. My car (from my grandma) needs repairs.
3. The clouds (under the rainbow) covered the mountain.

Suggested appositives are added between commas.

4. My favorite book, <u>Robinson Crusoe</u>, lay on the shelf.
5. The boy next door, Sam Miller, climbs our tree.

6. Susan, the lady in the blue dress, is an old friend.

Adjective clauses are in italics.

7. The school *that I attended* has closed.
8. The signed edition of <u>Tom Sawyer</u> *that my parents found* is quite valuable.
9. My brother, *who is well-known for his humor*, tricked me on April Fools' Day.
10. Our trip to England, *which was postponed last year*, is approaching soon.

EXERCISE B

Suggestions for an adverb or adverb phrase for each verb are given below.

The stars are shining *brightly*.

The car skidded *suddenly*.

We climbed the mountain *enthusiastically*.

1. The stars are shining *with intensity*.
2. The car skidded *with a sudden lurch*.
3. We climbed the mountain *with enthusiasm*.

The adverb phrases and clauses are in italics in the sentences below.

4. The garden was planted *in the spring*.
5. We harvested *during the summer*.
6. We took the crops *to market*.
7. *Because an ice storm hit last night*, stores and offices were closed.
8. I cleaned the house *while Mother slept*.
9. *Since I shopped for Christmas early*, I have all my gifts.
10. *When you have finished mowing the lawn*, please trim the hedge.

EXERCISES C & D

In the sentences below the following are identified: adjective (ADJ) and adverb (ADV) clauses, noun clauses (N), direct (DO) and indirect objects (IO), predicate nominatives (PN), and predicate adjectives (PA). Each sentence type is also identified.

1. The stone *which the builders rejected* (ADJ) has become the chief *cornerstone* (PN). cx

2. I will meditate on Your precepts and contemplate Your *ways* (DO). s

3. I see wondrous *things* (DO) from Your law. s

4. I am a *stranger* (PN) in the earth. s

5. (You) Give *me* (IO) *understanding* (DO), and I shall keep Your *law* (DO). cd

6. I shall observe *it* (DO) with my whole heart. s

7. I hope for Your salvation, and I do Your *commandments* (DO). cd

8. My soul keeps Your *testimonies* (DO), and *that I love them exceedingly* (N) is *true* (PA). cd-cx

9. The entirety of Your word is *truth* (pn), and every one of Your righteous judgments endures forever. cd

10. The LORD will be your *confidence* (PN). s

11. His truth shall be your *shield* and *buckler* (PN). s

12. He is my *refuge* and my *fortress* (PN). s

13. He is our *God*, and we are the *people* of His pasture, and the *sheep* of His hand (PN). cd

14. The LORD God is a *sun* and a *shield* (PN). s

15. The LORD will give *grace* and *glory* (DO) to *whoever cries out to Him* (N). cx

16. You were once *darkness*, but now you are *light* in the Lord (PN). cd

17. For we are *members* (PN) of His body. s

18. *That the husband is the head of the wife* (N) is taught in Scripture. cx

19. *When sin has conceived* (ADV), it gives birth (DO) to death. cx

20. *If any of you lacks wisdom* (ADV), ask God (DO). cx

21. *Blessed* (PA) is the man *who endures temptation* (ADJ). cx

22. *When he has been proved* (ADV), he will receive the *crown* (DO) of life *which the Lord has promised to those who love Him* (ADJ). cx

23. *When the chief shepherd appears* (ADV), you will receive the *crown* (DO) of glory *that does not fade away* (ADJ). cx

24. He *who has begun a good work in you* (ADJ) will complete *it* (DO) until the day of Jesus Christ. cx

25. This is the *disciple* (PN) *who testifies of these things* (ADJ). cx

26. His hope is *that you might believe.* (N)

EXERCISE E

1. My soul keeps Your testimonies, and that I love them exceedingly is true.

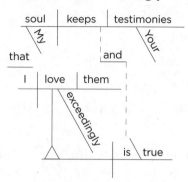

2. The entirety of Your word is truth, and every one of Your righteous judgments endures forever.

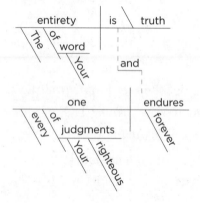

16. You were once darkness, but now you are light in the Lord.

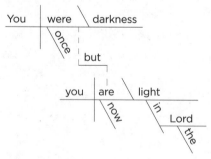

19. When sin has conceived, it gives birth to death.

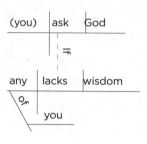

20. If any of you lacks wisdom, ask God.

UNIT 3
SPECIAL PROPERTIES OF NOUNS AND PRONOUNS

LESSON 28: TYPES OF NOUNS

EXERCISE A

Concrete nouns are listed with a (c), collective with a (col), and abstract with an (a).

retreat (c), duck (c), brood (col), pleasure (a), task (a), shells (c), visitors (c), canals (c), gossip (a), time (a)

LESSON 29: NUMBER

EXERCISE A

1. bushes, roofs, heroes, thieves
2. men, children, oxen, ladies
3. drive-ins, salmon, sheep, glasses
4. ships, sopranos, chiefs, pennies
5. potatoes, sons-in-law, cruises, wives

LESSON 30: GENDER

EXERCISE A

The gender of each of the noun is listed below.

1. bell (n), uncle (m), strawberry (n), girl (f), neighbor (c), sister (f), tree (n), rose (n), grass (n).
2. truth (n), goodness (n), clock (n), children (c), grandmother (f), soldier (m), people (c), statesman (m).
3. stag (m), landlady (f), heir (m), tiger (m), giant (m), countess (f), train (n), brook (n).
4. son (m), mare (f), lad (m), hero (m), czar (m), client (c), conductor (m), tailor (m), princess (f), book (n).

LESSON 31: CASE

EXERCISE A

1. Susan (n) returned the volleyballs (o) to the teacher (o).
2. The speaker (n) delivered the address (o) about femininity (o) to a large audience (o).
3. Lewis and Clark (n) were famous explorers (n) in the Northwest (o).
4. This is the finest restaurant (n) in the area (o).
5. The horse's (p) owner (n) was worried about the race (o).

EXERCISE B

1. Susan (s, f) returned the volleyballs (p, n) to the teacher (s, c).
2. The speaker (s, c) delivered the address (s, n) about femininity (s, f) to a large audience (s, c).
3. Lewis (s, m) and Clark (s, m) were famous explorers (p, c) in the Northwest (s, n).
4. This is the finest restaurant (s, n) in the area (s, n).
5. The horse's (s, c) owner (s, c) was worried about the race (s, n).

LESSON 32: THE DECLENSION OF A NOUN

EXERCISE A

1. child, children; child, children; child's, children's.
2. beauty, beauties; beauty, beauties; beauty's, beauties'.
3. tongue, tongues; tongue, tongues; tongue's, tongues'.
4. soil, soils; soil, soils; soil's, soils'.
5. family, families; family, families; family's, families'.

REVIEW EXERCISE A

Each italicized noun is followed by the type, number, gender, case, and usage.

1. The oldest settlement in our country is St. Augustine, Florida.
   settlement: common, singular, neuter, nominative, subject.
   St. Augustine: proper, singular, neuter, nominative, predicate nominative.
2. It was founded by the Spanish in 1595.
   Spanish: proper, plural, common, objective, object of the preposition.
3. The Frenchman Champlain planted a colony in Canada about forty years later where Quebec now stands.
   Frenchman: proper, singular, masculine, nominative, subject.
   colony: common, singular, neuter,

objective, direct object.

Canada: proper, singular, neuter, objective, object of preposition.

years: common, plural, neuter, objective, object of the preposition.

4. While on an expedition in New York state, Champlain discovered the lake that bears his name.

expedition: common, singular, neuter, objective, object of the preposition.

state: common, singular, neuter, objective, object of the preposition

Champlain: proper, singular, masculine, nominative, subject.

lake: common, singular, neuter, objective, direct object

name: common, singular, neuter, objective, direct object

LESSON 33: THE PERSONAL PRONOUN

EXERCISE A

The correct pronouns are in parentheses.

1. She knew it was (I).
2. She and (he) will go together.
3. May Liz and (I) leave now?
4. Mom expects you and (me) for dinner.
5. It was either (she) or her mother who answered the phone.
6. When will you and (they) come again?
7. Have you seen Mark and (him) together?
8. Not many could sing as well as (she).
9. This is the new mindset among (us) Americans.
10. Scott can run faster than (he).

EXERCISE B

The person (1, 2, 3), number (s, p), gender (m, f, c, n), and case (n, o, p) are listed in parentheses.

1. She (3, s, f, n) gives much time and money to her (3, s, f, p) favorite charities.
2. The boys ran through their (3, p, c, p) backyard to my (1, s, c, p) house.
3. He (3, s, m, n) received a letter from his (3, s, m, p) uncle.
4. Mother gave them (3, p, c, o) a much deserved spanking in her (3, s, f, p) bedroom.
5. They (3, p, c, n) will meet us (1, p, c, o) at our (1, p, c, p) boat dock.
6. It (3, s, n, n) is they (3, p, c, n) at the door now.
7. If he (3, s, m, n) bothers you (2, s, c, o) again, let me (1, s, c, o) know.
8. Give him (3, s, m, o) my (1, s, c, p) regards.
9. David and he (3, s, m, n) are regulars at the cafe.
10. The winners are Susan and she (3, s, f, n).

LESSON 34:
WHO, WHOM, WHOSE

EXERCISE A

The correct pronoun is in parentheses.

1. That is the woman (whom) we voted for. OR That is the woman for (whom) we voted.
2. That is the man (who) responded to my ad.
3. Do you know (who) I am?
4. My father is a person (whom) we all greatly admire.
5. Do you know (whom) the city is named after?
6. Famous American poets were among the writers (whom) we studied.

EXERCISE B

1. Whom do you mean?
2. Whom have we here?
3. Whom will you invite?
4. Whom did you give it to?
5. Who do you think I am?
6. Whom are you writing to?
7. Whom were you talking to?
8. Whom did she call?
9. I don't know whom to send.
10. Who was speaking to you?
11. I do not know whom he has met.
12. Who did you say sat beside you?
13. Who do you think will be elected?
14. Whom should I meet yesterday but my old friend Jones!
15. Who do you think called?
16. Whom do you know in your class?
17. You called whom at the office?
18. Give the invitations to whomever you wish.
19. Who is that woman?
20. He is going to be married to whom?

EXERCISE C

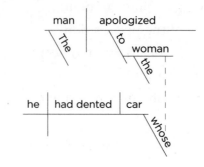

LESSON 35:
OTHER PRONOUNS

EXERCISE A

Interrogative (it), demonstrative (d), indefinite (id), or reflexive (r).

1. Whose is that? (it)
2. These are my mother's pearls. (d)
3. This is my old favorite. (d) Which is yours? (it)
4. Who do you think she is? (it)
5. What does that sign say? (it)
6. Each said his prayers. (id)
7. She said she would do it herself. (r)
8. Nobody could agree on a date. (id)
9. Several showed up late. (id)
10. Which would you like? (it)

LESSON 36:
PRONOUN AGREEMENT

EXERCISE A

1. After the concert, all of the students tried to get their programs signed by the performers.
2. Either Eric or Mark will be selected to read his short story.
3. Everyone in the college is expected to provide his own transportation.
4. Every ballerina was at her bar.
5. Each of the boarders has to do his own laundry.
6. Several of the instructors brought their wives.
7. Every choir member has his favorite piece.
8. Nobody in the cab had brought his wallet.
9. Katie and her sister were so late their father had begun to get worried.
10. Both boys brought their luggage with them to the museum.
11. If anyone calls while I am gone, please get his number.
12. None of the boys was able to call his parents.
13. Few of the preschoolers could tie their shoes.
14. Neither runner ran his best in the relay.
15. Robert and his brother bought their mountain bikes at the yard sale.
16. Everyone demanded his opinion be heard.
17. Neither Sue nor Tina ever answered her mail.
18. If anyone wants a free ticket, he must call today.
19. No one likes to find himself uninvited.
20. Neither of the baby birds could lift its wings.
21. A young man must make it his aim to excel.
22. Few of the dogs are obedient to their masters.

23. Some of the people were late to their appointments.
24. Emily or Laura will pick up her aunt and uncle at the airport.

EXERCISE B

The incorrect pronoun is in italics, followed by the correct pronoun.

1. *their*, his
2. Correct
3. *they*, he
4. Correct
5. *his*, its
6. *themself*, himself
7. *I*, me
8. *his*, their
9. *their*, her
10. *they*, you

LESSON 37: REVIEW

EXERCISE A

1. Proper nouns, common nouns, concrete nouns, abstract nouns, and collective nouns.
2. Number refers to how many things the noun names.
3. For the subject or a predicate nominative.
4. I, we, you, he, she, it, and they.
5. The objective case.
6. Masculine, feminine, common, and neuter.
7. The possessive case.
8. Nominative, objective, and possessive
9. Who, whom, whose, which, and what.
10. They are used to ask about someone or something of unknown identity.
11. This, that, these, and those.
12. Answers will vary.
13. They take the place of the subject of the sentence or clause, and they are used as direct objects, indirect objects, or objects of the preposition.

EXERCISE B

Answers will vary.

UNIT 4
SPECIAL PROPERTIES OF VERBS

LESSON 38: THE PRINCIPAL PARTS OF A VERB

EXERCISE A

Infinitive	Present	Past	Present Participle	Past Participle
to be	am/is/are	was	being	(have) been
to drink	drink	drank	drinking	(have) drunk
to come	come	came	coming	(have) come
to go	go/goes	went	going	(have) gone
to swim	swim	swam	swimming	(have) swum
to do	do	did	doing	(have) done
to blink	blink	blinked	blinking	have blinked
to bring	bring	brought	bringing	have brought
to choose	choose	chose	choosing	have chosen
to fly	fly	flew	flying	have flown
to see	see	saw	seeing	have seen
to eat	eat	ate	eating	have eaten
to write	write	wrote	writing	have written
to steal	steal	stole	stealing	have stolen
to throw	throw	threw	throwing	have thrown
to take	take	took	taking	have taken
to fall	fall	fell	falling	have fallen
to give	give	gave	giving	have given
to drive	drive	drove	driving	have driven
to speak	speak	spoke	speaking	have spoken
to pay	pay	paid	paying	have paid
to shrink	shrink	shrank	shrinking	have shrunk
to blow	blow	blew	blowing	have blown

to sink	sink	sank	sinking	have sunk
to know	know	knew	knowing	have known
to ring	ring	rang	ringing	have rung
to draw	draw	drew	drawing	have drawn
to find	find	found	finding	have found
to make	make	made	making	have made
to lay (put)	lay	laid	laying	have laid
to lie (rest)	lie	lay	lying	have lain
to have	have	had	having	have had
to raise	raise	raised	raising	have raised
to rise	rise	rose	rising	have risen

LESSON 40: ACTIVE AND PASSIVE VOICE

EXERCISE A

An A marks active; P marks passive. The verbs are identified in italics.

1. Eddie *grows* wheat on his farm in the Palouse. A
2. His family *has farmed* the same land for three generations. A
3. The land *has been plowed* and *planted* many times over the years. P
4. Wheat *is planted* in the spring and fall. P
5. Some years the farmers *harvest* the crop in early August. A
6. Other years the crop *is harvested* in late August. P
7. Heavy rains in late summer *can damage* the crop. A
8. The crop *can* also *be damaged* by late spring frosts. P
9. This year's crop *has* not *been harvested* yet. P
10. Passive verbs *can be recognized* easily. P

EXERCISE B

The original active sentence is followed by an example of a rewritten passive sentence.

1. I admire her voice. Her voice is admired by all.
2. Tulips covered the hillside. The hillside is covered with tulips.
3. The wind destroyed my garden. My garden was destroyed by the wind.

4. All the family enjoyed the barbecue. The barbecue was enjoyed by all the family.

5. I bought a new car last year. The car was purchased last year.

6. The skier crossed the wake with ease. The wake was easily crossed by the skier.

7. He took a picture of the old bridge. A picture of the old bridge was taken by him.

8. The boy mowed the lawn for his neighbor. The neighbor's lawn was mown by the boy.

9. The toddler picked the raspberries and ate them. The raspberries were picked and eaten by the toddler.

10. The rain left puddles on the sidewalk. Puddles were left on the sidewalk by the rain.

EXERCISE C

Conjugation of the verb *to see* in the passive voice.

Principal Parts

Infinitive	Present	Past	Present Participle	Past Participle
to see	see	saw	seeing	(have) seen

Present Tense

Singular	Plural
I am seen	we are seen
you are seen	you are seen
He, she, it is seen	they are seen

Present progressive: I am being seen

Past Tense

Singular	Plural
I was seen	we were seen
you were seen	you were seen
He, she, it was seen	they were seen

Past progressive: I was being seen

Future Tense

Singular	Plural
I shall be seen	we shall be seen
you will be seen	you will be seen
He, she, it will be seen	they will be seen

Future progressive: I shall be being seen

Present Perfect Tense

Singular	Plural
I have been seen	we have been seen
you have been seen	you have been seen
He, she, it has been seen	they have been seen

Present perfect progressive: I have been being seen

Past Perfect Tense (had + the past participle)

Singular	Plural
I had been seen	we had been seen
you had been seen	you had been seen
He, she, it had been seen	they had been seen

Past perfect progressive: I had been being seen

Future Perfect Tense (will have or shall have + past participle)

Singular	Plural
I shall have been seen	we shall have been seen
you will have been seen	you will have been seen
He, she, it will have been seen	they will have been seen

Future perfect progressive: I shall have been being seen

EXERCISE D

1. First person, plural, future, passive of *to praise*: We shall be praised.
2. Third person, singular, masculine, past perfect, active of *to sing*: He had sung.
3. Second person, plural, present, passive of *to love*: You are loved.
4. First person, singular, future perfect, passive of *to fly*: I shall have been flown.
5. Third person, plural, past, passive of *to see*: They were seen.
6. Third person, singular, feminine, present perfect, passive of *to take*: She has been taken.
7. Third person, singular, neuter, past, passive of *to eat*: It was eaten.

LESSON 41: MOOD

EXERCISE A

1. In the day of prosperity be joyful, but in the day of adversity consider. (imperative)
2. What profit has he who has labored for the wind? (indicative)
3. Forgive us our trespasses. (imperative)
4. Gather up the fragments that remain. (imperative)
5. I would remain here if you wish. (subjunctive)
6. He might improve, if he would make the effort. (subjunctive)
7. Depart from me, you workers of iniquity. (imperative)
8. Vanity of vanities, all is vanity. (indicative)
9. Better is a poor and wise youth than an old and foolish king who will be admonished no more. (indicative)
10. Fear God and keep His commandments, for this is the whole duty of man. (imperative)

LESSON 42: TRANSITIVE AND INTRANSITIVE VERBS

EXERCISE A

The transitivity of the verbs follows each sentence.

1. Cain killed Abel. (transitive)
2. John wrote a long letter to his brother. (transitive)
3. God made the world. (transitive)
4. She wept. (intransitive)
5. The bird sat very still on the branch. (intransitive)
6. She heard the clock ticking. (transitive)
7. Bill went home for summer vacation. (intransitive)
8. Mother closed the door. (transitive)
9. The child loves his mother. (transitive)
10. The kite rose gracefully in the wind. (intransitive)

EXERCISE C

The type of verb is given in parentheses, and its direct object is underlined (if there is one).

1. After the curtain descended (intransitive) on the final tableau, Redding waited (intransitive) in the lobby while the stream of people passed. (intransitive)
2. The Wiggses had obeyed (transitive) instructions, and were (linking) the very last to come out.
3. They seemed (linking) dazed by their recent glimpse into fairy-land.
4. Something in their thin bodies and pinched faces made Redding form (transitive) a sudden resolve.
5. "Billy," he said gravely, "can't you and your family take (transitive) supper with me?"

6. Billy and his mother exchanged (transitive) doubtful <u>glances</u>.
7. For the past three hours everything had been (linking) so strange and unusual that they were (linking) bewildered.

LESSON 43: SUBJECT-VERB AGREEMENT

EXERCISE A

Select the appropriate verb to agree with the subject in the following sentences.

1. One of the students (is) presenting a paper today.
2. Sally, along with many classmates, (is) signed up for the field trip.
3. Nobody in the class (wants) to miss it.
4. Everyone in the neighborhood (was) at the picnic.
5. Few (were) tardy today.
6. Some of my aunt's dishes (are) broken.
7. Some of my uncle's tobacco (is) missing.
8. (Are) any of you boys going to the gym?
9. (Is) there any reason for this?
10. Law and order (is) the need of the hour.
11. Mr. Jones and Mr. Jacobs (were) absent from the board meeting.
12. (Is) the salt and pepper on the table?
13. Neither hail nor sleet (was) expected.
14. Either the hall or the entryway (is) where I left the letter.
15. Either the dogs or the cat (is) making that noise.
16. The class (is) going skiing this weekend.
17. The cause of the destruction in my garden (is) the bunnies.
18. There (are) my cousins.
19. Six dollars (is) too much to pay.
20. Every car and bus (is) honking (its) horn.

LESSON 44: REVIEW

REVIEW QUESTIONS

1. Infinitive, present, past, present participle, past participle
2. to
3. Present participle and past participle
4. A regular verb forms the past and past participle by adding -ed or -d to the infinitive form. Irregular verbs change their spelling in various ways.
5. Swim, swim, swam, swimming, have swum
6. Present, past, future, present perfect, past perfect, future perfect
7. The verb ends in -s, as in sings.
8. Will have or shall have
9. The helping verbs have, has, or had
10. Past participle
11. The -ing form of the verb
12. To list the verb forms in all tenses, numbers, and persons.
13. When the subject is doing the action it is active voice; when the action is being done to the subject, it is passive voice.

14. Passive voice

15. I call, I am called

16. A transitive verb requires an object to complete the thought; an intransitive does not require an object.

17. Action verb

18. Helping verb, linking verb

19. The verb must always agree with its subject in number.

20. The subject

21. I, he, she, it, its, him, her, his, hers, each, either, neither, one, everyone, everybody, no one, nobody, anyone, anybody, someone, somebody.

22. We, they, them, us

23. Some, all, any, most, none

24. The prepositional phrase that modifies the pronoun determines the number.

25. Plural

26. We think of them as one thing.

27. Singular

28. The verb agrees in number with the subject nearer to the verb.

29. If the group is considered one unit, it requires a singular verb; if it suggests a collection of individuals acting separately, it is plural.

UNIT 5
VERBALS

LESSON 45:
PARTICIPLES

EXERCISE A

The participles are in italics below, and the noun each modifies is underlined.

1. We gave him an *illustrated* dinosaur <u>book</u> for his birthday.
2. The *winding* <u>road</u> led to our grandparents' home.
3. She hired a contractor to repair the *damaged* <u>roof</u>.
4. He wanted to grow up to become a *wandering* <u>minstrel</u>.
5. *Migrating* <u>geese</u> fly over our house each fall.
6. The *yelping* <u>puppies</u> tumbled out the door to greet our visitors.
7. The teacher addressed the *assembled* <u>class</u>.
8. My *disappointed* <u>daughter</u> held back her tears.
9. The *exhausted* relay <u>team</u> collapsed in the shade.
10. She looked with curiosity at the *forbidden* <u>box</u>.

EXERCISE B

The participial phrases are in italics in the sentences below.

1. The team, *tired from the heat*, finally won the championship game.
2. *Leading at half-time*, the team had felt confident.
3. The top scorer, *acclaimed for his quickness*, suffered an injury soon after the half.
4. The rest of the team, *wearied from several previous games*, knew they had to work harder.
5. *Plagued by more injuries and poor shots*, the team almost lost.

EXERCISE C

1. The singing choir marched onto the stage.

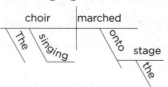

2. Scaling the wall, the convict nearly escaped.

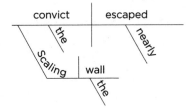

3. Offering her his hand, he helped her from the car.

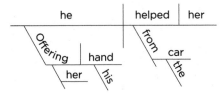

4. Seeing the large crowd gathered for the occasion, the speaker almost lost his nerve.

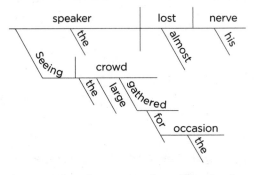

5. Annoyed at her own clumsiness, the rider got back on the frightened horse.

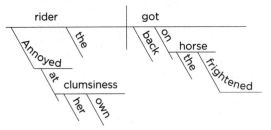

EXERCISE D

1. seeing   seen
2. speaking   spoken
3. weaving   woven
4. burning   burnt
5. growing   grown

EXERCISE E

Examples of rewritten sentences are given below.

1. Swaying dangerously, the huge tree finally gave way to the fierce wind.
2. The little boy was intrigued by the spider spinning his web.
3. We saw the moon rising above the hills just before midnight.
4. Insisting on our rights, we sometimes lose our sense of duty.
5. We saw the blue jay screaming and chattering in its nest.

LESSON 46: GERUNDS

EXERCISE A

The gerunds in the following sentences are in italics.

1. *Bobbing* for apples is an old-fashioned fall pastime.
2. He won by *running* the last lap full speed.
3. *Swinging* makes her dizzy.
4. The people love the *preaching* at that church.
5. The doctor's chief concern is her erratic *breathing*.

EXERCISE B

The gerunds and gerund phrases in the following sentences are in italics, and their function in the sentence follows.

1. My mother delights in *baking cookies for her grandchildren*. (object of preposition)
2. *Cleaning the oven* is not my favorite task. (subject)
3. By *printing a retraction*, the error was corrected. (object of preposition)
4. *Forgiving those who wrong you* may be difficult, but it is necessary. (subject)
5. Something that I have always enjoyed is *hanging wallpaper*. (predicate nominative)
6. My vacation last year, *visiting my aunt in Hawaii*, will be hard to top. (appositive)
7. By *gossiping about her friends*, she has created much havoc. (object of preposition)
8. I dislike *playing the accordion*. (direct object)
9. *Listening to the clock chime* is a joy to my grandson. (subject)
10. She loves *surfing and scuba diving in the summer*. (direct object)

EXERCISE C

1. He earned money during the summer by mowing lawns.

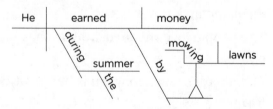

2. His latest hobby is collecting old coins.

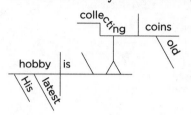

3. Painting old furniture is her full-time job.

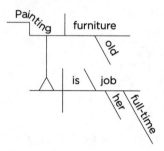

4. The children love singing in the church choir.

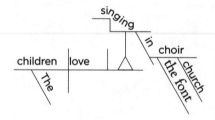

5. Her assignment, writing several poems, was both difficult and enjoyable.

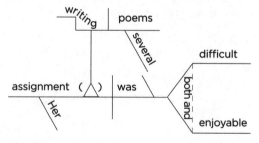

LESSON 47: INFINITIVES

EXERCISE A

Each infinitive is in italics followed by how it is used (as noun, adjective, or adverb).

1. This is weather *to watch* (adj) carefully.
2. I want *to learn* (n) *to skate* (n).*
3. The young boy tried *to read* (n) the sign.
4. The plane is ready *to take off*† (adv).
5. The mechanic *to call* (adj) is Pete.
6. I want *to tell* (n) you the truth.
7. Learn *to do* (n) good.
8. *To obey* (n) is better than sacrifice.
9. They are in a hurry *to leave* (adj).
10. That was a day *to remember* (adj).

EXERCISE B

The infinitives or infinitive phrases in the following sentences are in italics followed by how the infinitive is used (noun, adjective, or adverb). Nouns are followed by how they are used in the sentence.

1. She is a pleasure *to know* (adj).
2. We are excited *to go on our trip* (adv).‡
3. This salsa is too hot for me! No infinitive in this sentence.
4. *To succeed*, you must work hard (adv).§

* The first infinitive, *to learn*, is the direct object of *want* (*want what? To learn*). The second infinitive, *to skate*, is the direct object of the first infinitive, *learn* (*learn what? to skate*).
† *Take off* is a phrasal verb.
‡ The infinitive phrase modifies the adjective *excited*.
§ The infinitive modifies the adverb *hard*.

5. I like *to spend my vacation time at home* (n; do).
6. She is hoping *to pass her test* (n; do).
7. The boys are ready *to go* (adv). ¶
8. The baby in the tub is so fun *to watch* (adv).**
9. *To find the time to exercise* is hard for me (n; s).
10. Do you want *to go* to the show with me? (n; do)

EXERCISE C

1. Take time to do well.

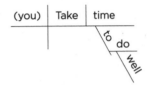

2. To do well is not easy for the lazy.

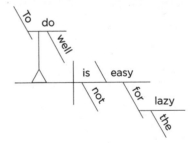

3. It is hard for them to have a thankless child.

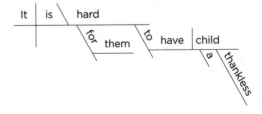

¶ The infinitive modifies the adjective *ready*.
** The infinitive modifies the adjective *fun*.

4. She went to explore ancient ruins in Mexico before she came to Peoria to marry Bob.

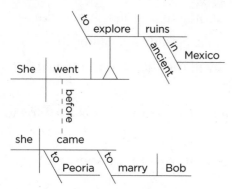

5. He has the ability to win the race.

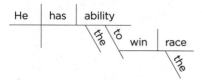

REVIEW EXERCISE A

1. Racing down the hill, I tried to catch the runaway pony, but he disappeared into the woods before I could reach him.

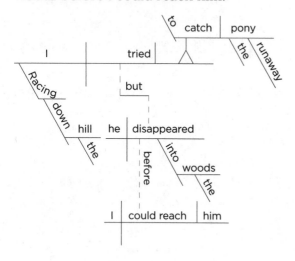

2. The disappointed crowd is hoping to see the show if the audio can be repaired.

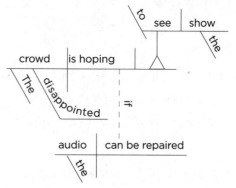

3. Believing that elves and fairies lived in these hills was once common among the plain folk.

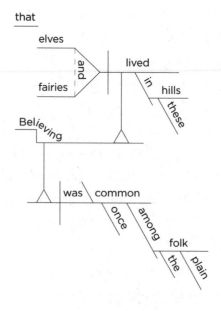

UNIT 6
SPECIAL PROPERTIES
OF MODIFIERS

LESSON 48:
ADJECTIVES
AND ADVERBS,
COMPARATIVES AND
SUPERLATIVES

EXERCISE A

The comparatives and superlatives are listed below. Those that cannot be compared are left blank.

	Comparative	Superlative
1.	better	best
2.	richer	richest
3.	more virtuous	most virtuous
4.	_____	_____
5.	more destructive	most destructive
6.	straighter	straightest
7.	rounder	roundest
8.	stronger	strongest
9.	more robust	most robust
10.	more sincere	most sincere
11.	lower	lowest
12.	swifter	swiftest
13.	more grateful	most grateful
14.	more studious	most studious
15.	littler	littlest
16.	more extensive	most extensive
17.	more slowly	most slowly
18.	more rapid	most rapid
19.	sooner	soonest
20.	more sweetly	most sweetly
21.	merrier	merriest
22.	more brilliant	most brilliant
23.	whiter	whitest

EXERCISE B

The adjectives and adverbs in the sentences are underlined and the degree of comparison of each is listed.

1. Tomorrow promises to be the <u>most glorious</u> day. (superlative)
2. The sun is <u>more brilliant</u> than the moon. (comparative)
3. That was the <u>best</u> rehearsal so far. (superlative)
4. What a <u>merry</u> little tune that was. (positive)
5. The shadows are growing <u>longer</u>. (comparative)

EXERCISE C

The sentences are rewritten with corrections in italics with corrections.

1. Which of the two books do you like *better*?
2. The yard *looks lovelier* than it ever has before.
3. I prefer eating at Swilly's than *eating at* Bonanza.
4. Correct
5. This book is older than all the *other* books in the library.

LESSON 49: DANGLING OR MISPLACED MODIFIERS

EXERCISE A

Sample rewritten sentences:

1. She wanted to bake cookies with frosting and sprinkles for the party.
2. While I was practicing the trumpet, the neighbor's dog began howling.
3. When we had driven several blocks, the tailgate flew open.
4. I almost ran over the woman in the large hat with her poodle.
5. While Mom was baking the bread, the house smelled good.